LOOKING AT LITERATURE

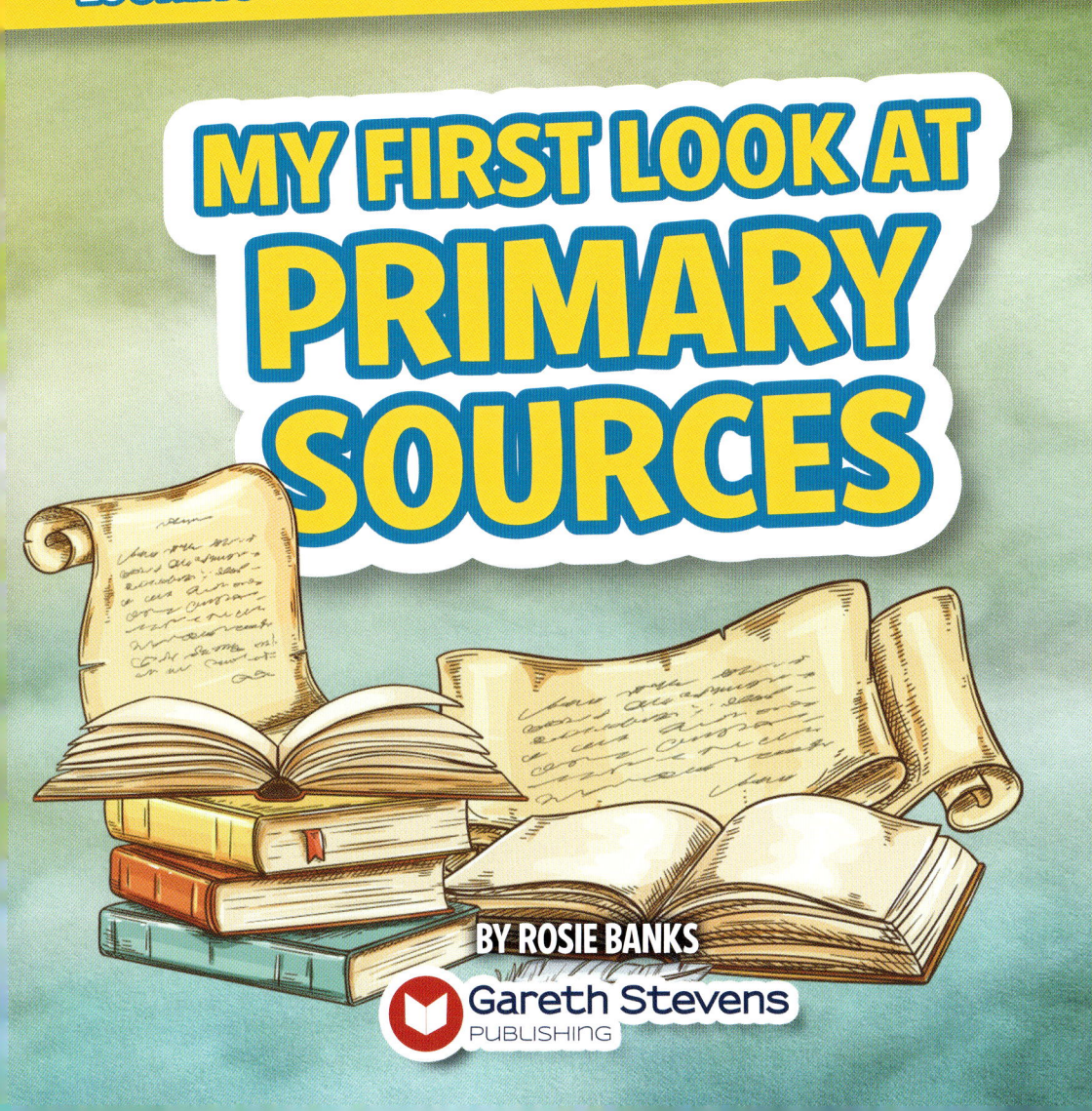

MY FIRST LOOK AT PRIMARY SOURCES

BY ROSIE BANKS

Gareth Stevens
PUBLISHING

Please visit our website, www.garethstevens.com. For a free color catalog of all our high-quality books, call toll free 1-800-542-2595 or fax 1-877-542-2596.

Library of Congress Cataloging-in-Publication Data

Names: Banks, Rosie 1978- author.
Title: My first look at primary sources / Rosie Banks.
Description: New York : Gareth Stevens Publishing, [2022] | Series: Looking at literature | Includes index.
Identifiers: LCCN 2020029575 (print) | LCCN 2020029576 (ebook) | ISBN 9781538264119 (library binding) | ISBN 9781538264096 (paperback) | ISBN 9781538264102 (6 pack) | ISBN 9781538264126 (ebook)
Subjects: LCSH: History–Sources–Juvenile literature. | History–Research–Juvenile literature. | Information resources–Juvenile literature.
Classification: LCC D5.5 .B36 2022 (print) | LCC D5.5 (ebook) | DDC 907.2–dc23
LC record available at https://lccn.loc.gov/2020029575
LC ebook record available at https://lccn.loc.gov/2020029576

Published in 2022 by
Gareth Stevens Publishing
111 East 14th Street, Suite 349
New York, NY 10003

Copyright © 2022 Gareth Stevens Publishing

Designer: Rachel Rising
Editor: Kate Mikoley

Photo credits: Cover, p.1 Vector Tradition/Shutterstock.com; Cover, p.1 Dmitry Karlov/Shutterstock.com; Cover, p. 1 Larissa Kulik/Shutterstock.com; pp. 3, 4, 6, 8, 10, 12, 14, 16, 18, 20, 21, 22, 23, 24 (background) carduus/DigitalVision Vectors/Getty Images; p. 5 Glowimages/Getty Images; p. 7 Ken Kiefer 2/Cultura/Getty Images; p. 9 Heritage Images/ Hulton Archive/Getty Images; p. 11 AAMIR QURESHI/Staff/AFP/Getty Images; p. 13 Francis Miller/The LIFE Picture Collection/Getty Images; pp. 15, 19 Library of Congress/Corbis Historical/Getty Images; p. 17 Buyenlarge/Archive Photos/Getty Images; p. 20 Clarissa Leahy/Cultura/Getty Images; p. 21 Edgardo Contreras/Photodisc/Getty Images.

All rights reserved. No part of this book may be reproduced in any form without permission in writing from the publisher, except by a reviewer.

Printed in the United States of America

Some of the images in this book illustrate individuals who are models. The depictions do not imply actual situations or events.

CPSIA compliance information: Batch #CSGS22: For further information contact Gareth Stevens, New York, New York at 1-800-542-2595.

Find us on

CONTENTS

Pick the Primary Source............... 4
Diaries............................. 8
Autobiographies 10
Speeches........................... 12
Interviews......................... 14
More Written Sources 16
Tech Today......................... 18
So Many More...................... 20
Your Turn!......................... 21
Glossary........................... 22
For More Information............... 23
Index.............................. 24

Boldface words appear in the glossary.

Pick the Primary Source

Imagine you missed a friend's party. You want to know what happened. Would you ask another person who wasn't there about it? It would be much better to ask someone who went to the party. That person is a primary source of **information**.

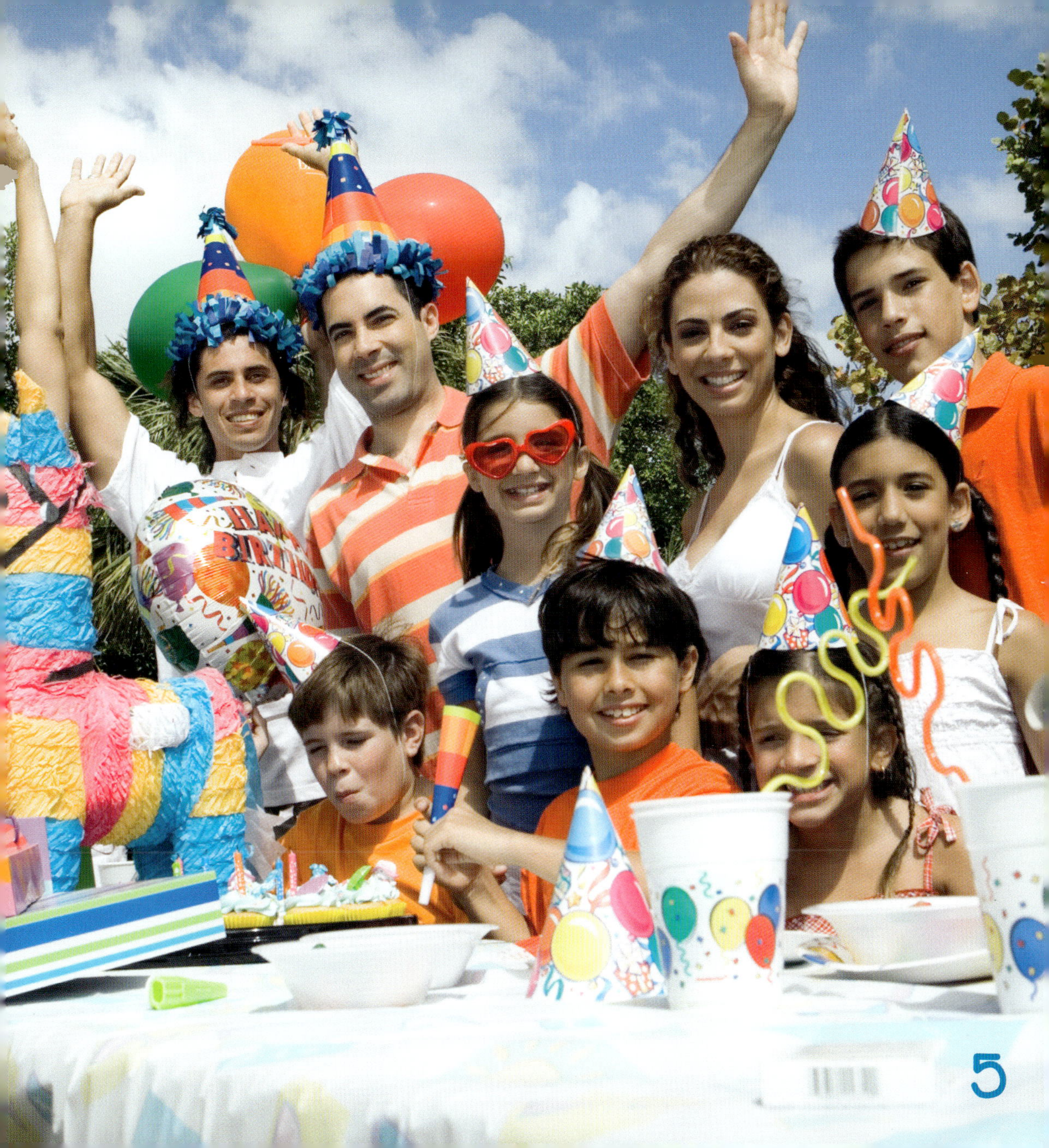

A primary source gives a **firsthand** report about something. That means it comes from someone who was there. For example, a **photograph** is a primary source. It shows a picture of a time and place. Primary sources help us learn about history.

7

Diaries

People write diaries to remember their thoughts and **experiences**. A young Jewish girl named Anne Frank wrote a diary during **World War II**. She and her family hid from **Nazis**, who wanted to hurt them. Her diary is a primary source of this time.

In het kamertje met Kitty en twee jongens waaronder Bernd aan theetafel bezig dan op school onweg door een storm heen kinderen en allerlei diverse tonelen b.v. in bed met vader en aan tafel.
3e Deel. Anne haar toiletten de P. mevr. .... fietsen ijsjurk die cadeau zo een witte en schoenen.

bergen en De Louteringskuur, zo lijken me wel leuk. De Opstandelingen heeft ze ook meegebracht. Dat is van Ammers Küller. Dezelfde schrijfster als van Heeren, Vrouwen, Knechten. Dit mag ik nu ook lezen. Dan heb ik een hele boel liefde's romantoneelen van Körner gelezen, ik vind dat die man leuk schr. B.v. Hedwig, der Vetter aus Bremen, Hans Heilings Felsen, Der Grüne Domino, Die Gouvernante, Der Vierjährige Posten, Die Sühne, Der kamf mit dem Drachen, Der Nachtwächter en zoal meer. Vader wil dat ik nu ook Hebbel en andere boeken van andere welbekende Duitse schrijvers ga lezen. Het Duits lezen gaat nu al betrekkelijk vlot. Alleen fluister ik het meestal, in plaats dat ik zelf lees. Maar dat gaat wel over.

Dit is een foto, zoals ik me zou wensen, altijd zo te zijn. Dan had ik nog wel een kans om naar Holywood te komen. Maar tegenwoordig zie ik er jammer genoeg meestal anders uit.
Annefrank.
10 Oct.

Autobiographies

An autobiography is the story of someone's life written by that person. Malala Yousafzai is a young woman from Pakistan who fought for girls' right to go to school. Her autobiography is a primary source that tells us about the dangers she faced.

I AM MALALA

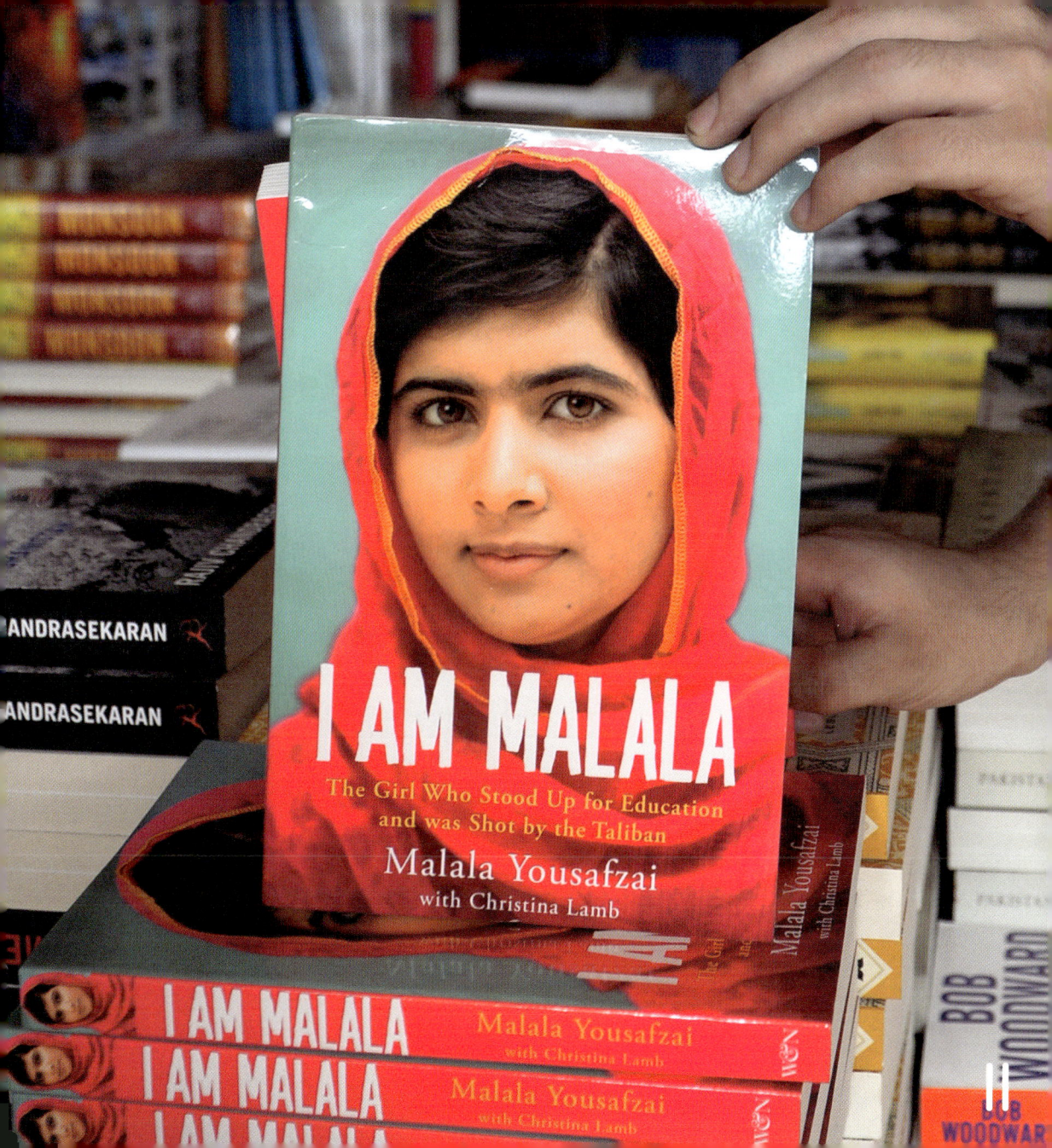

The Girl Who Stood Up for Education and was Shot by the Taliban

Malala Yousafzai
with Christina Lamb

Speeches

Speeches are also primary sources. We can read and sometimes hear and watch them. Famous leaders give speeches. In 1963, Martin Luther King Jr. gave a speech in Washington, DC. He talked about his dream of equality and freedom for Black Americans.

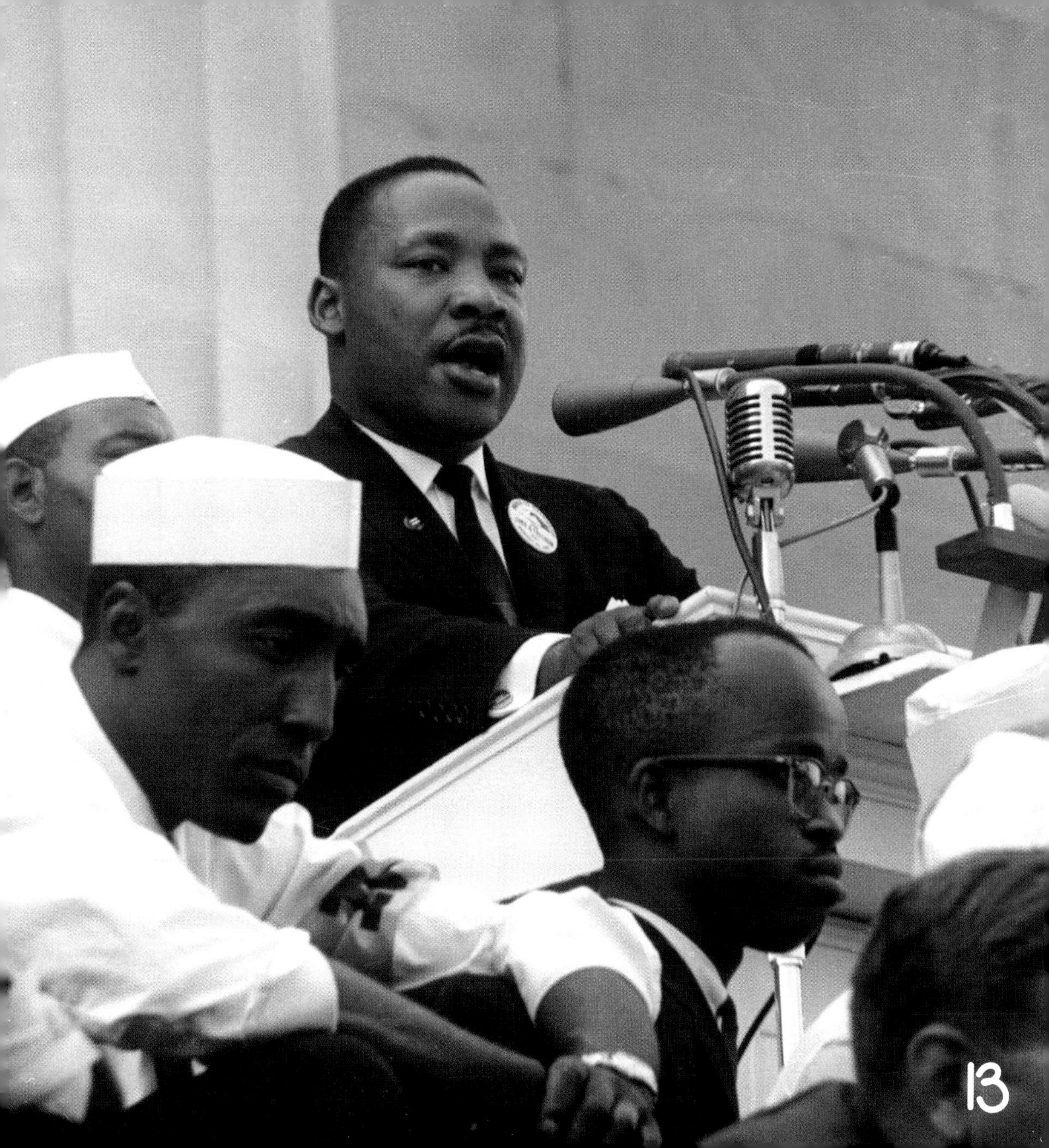

Interviews

Interviewing people is another way to gather primary source information. From 1936 to 1938, the U.S. government interviewed people who had been enslaved. Reading their experiences is a good way to learn about these people's lives. Interviews can be recorded too.

15

More Written Sources

Letters, newspapers, and laws are more examples of written primary sources. The highest law in the United States is the U.S. Constitution. This primary source was written in 1787. We read it to understand U.S. government and laws. It's found in Washington, DC.

17

Tech Today

Technology has given us more primary sources. We can listen and watch things happen with sound and **video** recordings. For example, recordings of Native Americans help us learn about native peoples' languages. Some of these languages are no longer spoken.

19

So Many More

Maps, clothes, tools, and buildings are just a few more primary sources. Emails and other online messages are primary sources too. All these will help people in the future understand more about events of the past and today!

Your Turn!

Interview a grandparent or other older person. Ask questions about what life was like when they were young. Write down the answers. Share your primary source with a friend.

GLOSSARY

experience: something someone has done or that has happened to them

firsthand: coming from seeing or experiencing something for oneself

information: facts about a subject

interview: to meet with someone to ask questions in order to get information about something. Also, the meeting at which questions are asked.

Nazi: a member of a German political party that controlled Germany from 1933 to 1945, led by Adolph Hitler

photograph: a picture made by a camera

technology: a machine, piece of equipment, or method created by people as useful tools and to solve problems

video: an event that has been recorded so that it can be watched on a TV or computer screen

World War II: a war fought from 1939 to 1945 in many countries around the world

FOR MORE INFORMATION

BOOKS

Boswell, Kelly. *Research Primary Source Documents: Diaries, Letters, Journals, and More!* North Mankato, MN: Pebble, 2019.

Keller, Susanna. *What Are Primary Sources?* New York, NY: Britannica Educational Publishing, 2019.

Tait, Leia. *Primary Sources.* New York, NY: AV^2 by Weigl, 2020.

WEBSITES

Kid-Friendly Primary Sources
dppl.org/blog/post/kid-friendly-primary-sources
Take a look at some primary sources.

Primary Sources: A Research Guide
umb.libguides.com/PrimarySources/secondary
Learn more about primary sources as well as what secondary sources are.

Publisher's note to educators and parents: Our editors have carefully reviewed these websites to ensure that they are suitable for students. Many websites change frequently, however, and we cannot guarantee that a site's future contents will continue to meet our high standards of quality and educational value. Be advised that students should be closely supervised whenever they access the Internet.

INDEX

autobiographies 10

buildings 20

clothes 20

diaries 8

emails 20

Frank, Anne 8

interviews 14, 21

King, Martin Luther Jr. 12

laws 16

letters 16

maps 20

newspapers 16

photographs 6

recordings 14, 18

speeches 12

technology 18

tools 20

U.S. Constitution 16

World War II 8

Yousafzai, Malala 10